# DON'T STEP
## IN THE
# LEADERSHIP

# DON'T STEP
## IN THE
# LEADERSHIP

**A DILBERT® BOOK**

BY **SCOTT ADAMS**

**Andrews McMeel**
**Publishing**

Kansas City

DILBERT® is a registered trademark of United Feature Syndicate, Inc.

DOGBERT and DILBERT appear in the comic strip DILBERT®, distributed by United Feature Syndicate, Inc.

www.dilbert.com

www.andrewsmcmeel.com

99 00 01 02 03 BAH 10 9 8 7 6 5 4 3 2 1

ISBN: 0-8362-7844-5

Library of Congress Catalog Card Number: 98-88670

For Puzzle Girl

# Other DILBERT books from Andrews McMeel Publishing

## Journey to Cubeville
ISBN: 0-8362-7175-0  hardcover
ISBN: 0-8362-6745-1  paperback

## I'm Not Anti-Business, I'm Anti-Idiot
ISBN: 0-8362-5182-2

## Seven Years of Highly Defective People
ISBN: 0-8362-5129-6  hardcover
ISBN: 0-8362-3668-8  paperback

## Casual Day Has Gone Too Far
ISBN: 0-8362-2899-5

## Fugitive from the Cubicle Police
ISBN: 0-8362-2119-2

## Still Pumped from Using the Mouse
ISBN: 0-8362-1026-3

## It's Obvious You Won't Survive by Your Wits Alone
ISBN: 0-8362-0415-8

## Bring Me the Head of Willy the Mailboy!
ISBN: 0-8362-1779-9

## Shave the Whales
ISBN: 0-8362-1740-3

## Dogbert's Clues for the Clueless
ISBN: 0-8362-1737-3

## Build a Better Life by Stealing Office Supplies
ISBN: 0-8362-1757-8

## Always Postpone Meetings with Time-Wasting Morons
ISBN: 0-8362-1758-6

**For ordering information, call 1-800-642-6480.**

# Introduction

Everyone says there's a lack of leadership in the world these days. I think we should all be thankful, because the only reason for leadership is to convince people to do things that are either dangerous (like invading another country) or stupid (working extra hard without extra pay).

Obviously you don't need any leadership to lead you to, for example, eat a warm cookie. But you need a lot of leadership to convince you to march through a desert and shoot strangers. Generally speaking, whenever there is leadership, there is lots of hollering and very few warm cookies. Let's enjoy the lack of leadership while we have it.

Unfortunately, whenever there's a void, someone always fills it. We don't want someone evil being the leader, so I recommend filling the job with a cartoonist. I'd be willing to give it a go. Like any leader, I'll try to get people to do things that are dangerous and stupid, but my plan is to make those things funny for the people who aren't directly involved. That's the best you can hope for when it comes to leadership.

For example, I would limit CEO compensation to whatever the CEO can carry away in his cheeks like a squirrel every night.

To shorten business meetings, I would authorize the invention of special chairs that heat up ten degrees for every minute the occupant talks. If you can make your point in one minute, you get a nicely warmed chair. But if you ramble on for forty minutes, you'll burst into flames to the delight and applause of the other attendees.

I would also encourage a modified version of Scrabble rules for business meetings. If someone uses an acronym or buzzword that sounds suspicious, you can challenge him to define it. If the offender can't define the word, he loses his job. But if he can, he gets to slap the challenger with an appointment calendar.

That's just a sample of the leadership I would provide. This book will give you a good idea of what else is on my agenda. But I consider my leadership temporary, anticipating the day when Dogbert conquers the planet and forces into domestic service everyone who opposed him. You can avoid that fate by joining Dogbert's New Ruling Class (DNRC) now and getting on his good side. All you need to do is sign up for the free *Dilbert* newsletter and you're in the DNRC.

To subscribe, send an e-mail to listserv@listserv.unitedmedia.com in the following format:

subject: newsletter
message: Subscribe Dilbert_News Firstname Lastname

Don't include any other information—your e-mail address will be picked up automatically.

If the automatic method doesn't work for you, you can also subscribe by writing to scottadams@aol.com or via snail mail:

Dilbert Mailing List
United Media
200 Madison Avenue
New York, NY 10016

These methods are much slower than the automatic method so please be patient.

S.Adams

Scott Adams

BLIND PEOPLE OFTEN HAVE EXCELLENT HEARING. THE BRAIN COMPENSATES FOR ANY LOST FUNCTION BY BOLSTERING OTHERS.

IN ALL LIKELIHOOD, RATBERT, YOU'RE SO DUMB THAT YOU HAVE TELEKINETIC POWER.

WOW!

I HAVE THE POWER TO WATCH TELEVISION!

I WILL DEBUNK YOUR LUDICROUS CLAIM OF PSYCHIC ABILITY WITH ONE HUNDRED FLIPS OF THIS COIN.

CALL IT.

EDGE.

THAT IS JUST A COINCIDENCE.

I CALL EDGE FOR THE NEXT 99 TOO.

JUST BECAUSE YOU GUESSED A HUNDRED COIN FLIPS IN A ROW DOESN'T MEAN YOU'RE PSYCHIC. COINCIDENCES DO HAPPEN.

I CALL SEVEN ROTATIONS FOLLOWED BY INEXPLICABLE HOVERING AND HEN NOISES.

THAT IS LUCK... LUCK, LUCK, LUCK, LUCK, LUCK!

ARE WE DONE NOW?

IS THIS THE "SKEPTICS ASSOCIATION"?

I NEED YOUR HELP TO PROVE MY RAT ISN'T PSYCHIC.

MY NAME IS DILBERT.

YES, I CAN PROVE IT; I HAVE A PASSPORT AND A DRIVER'S LICENSE.

WELL, YEAH, IT'S EASY TO GET A FAKE ID, BUT...

HOURS LATER...

...OKAY, WHAT IF I TAKE A DNA TEST?

NO, I CAN'T PROVE I'VE NEVER BEEN CLONED!!

I'M GLAD THE "SKEPTICS ASSOCIATION" SENT YOU TO DEBUNK MY RAT'S CLAIMS OF ESP.

THE OTHERS DON'T GO OUT MUCH SINCE THEIR BAD EXPERIENCES AS JURORS ON THE O.J. SIMPSON TRIAL.

WELL, I'M GLAD YOU COULD MAKE IT.

LET'S HURRY. I HAVE TO DEBUNK THE SO-CALLED HUBBLE TELESCOPE LATER TODAY.

KEN THE SKEPTIC...

I ALONE KNOW THE CONTENTS OF THIS ENVELOPE.

IT'S A CHARCOAL DRAWING OF A WOODCHUCK EATING A SMALL ORANGE.

NICE TRY, YOU LITTLE FRAUD, BUT THAT'S A LONG WAY FROM AN INK DRAWING OF A BEAVER EATING A TANGERINE.

I'VE USED THE SCIENTIFIC METHOD TO DEBUNK 100% OF THE PEOPLE WHO CLAIM THEY HAVE MENTAL POWERS.

ARE YOU SAYING THAT EVERY TEST YOU PERFORM TURNS OUT THE WAY YOU PREDICT IT WILL?

WHAT'S YOUR POINT?

YOU'VE PROVEN THAT YOU'RE PSYCHIC!!

**DOGBERT AND THE SKEPTIC**

IF YOUR CONTROLLED TESTS HAVE NEVER FOUND PSYCHIC POWERS, HOW DO YOU KNOW THE TESTS WORK FOR THAT SORT OF THING?

ISN'T THAT LIKE USING A METAL DETECTOR TO FIND OUT IF THERE ARE UNICORNS IN YOUR SOCK DRAWER?

NO!

LATER THAT NIGHT

A SKEPTIC CHECKS ALL THE DRAWERS.

THE SALES FORCE WAS OFFERED A RETIREMENT BUYOUT PACKAGE OF FIFTY DOLLARS.

ONE HUNDRED PERCENT OF THE SALES FORCE ELECTED TO TAKE THE OFFER.

I WONDER WHAT THEY KNOW THAT I DON'T KNOW.

THERE'S A HOLE WITH NO BOTTOM.

14

DEPUTY OF COMMON SENSE

ARE YOU THE GOVERNMENT SAFETY INSPECTOR?

YUP. I LOVE MY JOB.

WATCH YOUR STEP!

HEY!

HOW DOES YOUR BOSS DETERMINE YOUR PAY?

IT'S BASED ON THE DECREASE IN ACCIDENTS AFTER MY INSPECTION.

MAYBE I SHOULD QUIT AND WORK FOR MYSELF FROM HOME.

I WOULD MISS ALL THE HUMAN CONTACT.

SAME AS NOW.

I'M TESTING MY E-MAIL. DID YOU GET THE "E" I SENT?

I'M THINKING OF QUITTING AND WORKING FOR MYSELF.

COME WORK FOR ME.

DOING WHAT?

YOU'LL INVENT VALUABLE THINGS AND I'LL EXPLOIT YOU ... I MEAN THEM.

I'M NOT SURE YOU'D BE THE BEST BOSS, DOGBERT.

DON'T GIVE ME THAT INPUT, YOU "RESOURCE."

**WARNING!!**

AUTHOR NORMAN SOLOMON HAS DETERMINED THAT THE DILBERT COMIC STRIP IS HARMFUL TO WORKERS.

I WILL DEMONSTRATE THE DANGER WITH THIS CAREFULLY CONTROLLED EXPERIMENT.

HAVE YOUR PLANS FOR REBELLION BEEN REPLACED BY SARCASM AND COMPLACENCY?

AND I THINK I'M GOING BALD!

MY NEW POLICY IS TO DISCRIMINATE AGAINST SINGLE PEOPLE. IT'S TOTALLY LEGAL!

WRITE YOUR MARITAL STATUS ON THIS LIST, SO I KNOW WHO HAS NO REASON TO GO HOME AT NIGHT.

DANG! WHAT ARE THE ODDS YOU'D ALL BE POLYGAMISTS?

I'D LIKE TO TALK ABOUT MY CAREER PATH.

OKAY.

MY PLAN IS TO WORK YOU UNTIL YOUR HEALTH DETERIORATES AND YOUR SKILLS ARE OBSOLETE. THEN I'LL DOWNSIZE YOU.

I'M ILL.

REALLY? I'VE NEVER HAD A PLAN WORK THIS FAST BEFORE.

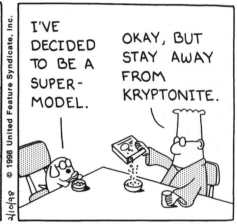

FASHION HEADQUARTERS

YOU COULD BE OUR NEXT SUPERMODEL. I LOVE THE TUMOR.

IT'S A BEAUTY MARK.

WE PREFER OUR SUPERMODELS TO LOOK UNHEALTHY, IN A SEXY WAY.

OKAY, IT'S A TUMOR.

I CAN ADD A FEW MORE. IT'S JUST "SILLY PUTTY."

NO, IT WOULD BE EASY TO OVERDO THAT SORT OF THING.

DOGBERT THE SUPERMODEL

YOUR FIRST ASSIGNMENT IS A LINGERIE SHOOT. YOU'LL BE WEARING BLACK SOCKS.

THERE'S NOTHING SEXIER THAN A SHORT, ROUND GUY IN BLACK SOCKS.

WOW! THIS WORKS!

QUICK! GET ME A BIG BLOCK OF ICE TO SIT ON!

HOW DOES IT FEEL TO BE A SEX SYMBOL?

GOOD.

PLAYGIRL IN SOCKS!

I REALIZED THAT WHAT'S INSIDE A PERSON DOESN'T COUNT BECAUSE NO ONE CAN SEE IT.

I DIDN'T REALIZE YOU WERE SUCH A PHILOSOPHER.

THAT'S MY POINT!

21

I FINISHED THE TECHNICAL RECOMMENDATION YOU REQUESTED.

AT FIRST I WAS MIFFED THAT YOU TOLD ME WHAT RECOMMENDATION YOU WANTED.

IT MADE ME FEEL USELESS AND WEAK.

BUT RATHER THAN DWELL ON MY POWERLESSNESS...

I DECIDED TO FIND JOY IN THE ONE DECISION I <u>CAN</u> MAKE.

I CHOSE A HELVETICA TYPE FONT.

AND I NEVER LOOKED BACK.

OH, SO THAT'S WHAT'S WRONG WITH IT.

I COACH AND I COACH, BUT THEY STILL WALK OUT OF HERE ALL RUBBER-LEGGED.

I'VE BEEN CHOSEN FOR THE INDUSTRIAL ESPIONAGE PROGRAM.

THE PLAN IS THAT I QUIT THIS JOB AND GO TO WORK FOR OUR COMPETITOR. EVERY WEEK I'LL SEND BACK SECRET REPORTS.

BOB, THIS IS HOW WE FIRE DUMB PEOPLE.

THAT'S WHY IT'S THE PERFECT COVER.

---

CATBERT: EVIL H.R. DIRECTOR

THE COMPANY'S GOAL IS TO DOUBLE THE EFFICIENCY OF ALL EMPLOYEES.

QUESTION: IF WE DOUBLE OUR EFFICIENCY, WON'T YOU DOWNSIZE HALF OF US?

DON'T TALK TO ANYONE IN MARKETING; THEY AREN'T SO GOOD AT MATH.

---

I'M GOING TO MAKE AN INFOMMERCIAL.

I'M TARGETING THE PEOPLE WHO WANT TO INVEST THEIR SAVINGS BUT DON'T KNOW HOW.

I HOPE YOU PLAN TO SELL EDUCATIONAL INFORMATION ABOUT HOW TO AVOID SCAMS.

GOOD IDEA FOR PHASE TWO!

26

...AND THE "DOGBERT CURSE" STRIKES ANYONE WHO SENDS A CHAIN LETTER. BUT THE LETTER SAID I'D DIE IF I DIDN'T.

YOU'RE THE WORLD'S SMARTEST GARBAGE MAN; HOW WOULD YOU HANDLE THIS?

DID YOU KNOW THERE'S ALSO A "GARBAGE MAN'S CURSE" FOR PEOPLE WHO SEND CHAIN LETTERS?

ARE YOU THE VICTIM OF A CURSE?

YES, I AM.

NEXT ON "20/20," JOHN STOSSEL SHOWS YOU THE CURE.

HA! AFTER THE COMMERCIAL I WILL GET VALUABLE INFORMATION FOR PEOPLE LIKE ME!

WELL, WELL. IT SEEMS MY OLD NEMESIS, JOHN STOSSEL, HAS BEEN BUSY.

OUR NEW SLOGAN IS, "PRESSURE MAKES DIAMONDS."

HOW ABOUT, "PRESSURE MAKES GARBAGE MORE COMPACT"? I WONDER IF THAT ONE IS TAKEN.

I HATE THIS STRONG JOB MARKET FOR ENGINEERS.

"IRRITATION MAKES PEARLS." OR MAYBE "PRESSURE MAKES WHINE."

28

**Panel 1:** I NEED HELP ON THE ASSIGNMENT THAT YOU SAID IS A "NO BRAINER."

**Panel 2:** IT'S EASY. JUST SKIP THE "INTERFACE DESIGN" PHASE AND MAKE EVERYTHING BEIGE. YOU CAN'T GO WRONG WITH BEIGE.

**Panel 3:** I ALWAYS KNOW WHERE TO GO FOR NO-BRAINER DECISIONS.

**Panel 4:** PROJECT STATUS. DUE TO BUDGET CUTS, OUR NEW PRODUCT WILL HAVE NO USER INTERFACE.

**Panel 5:** OUR TARGET MARKET IS PEOPLE WHO ARE TOO SHY TO RETURN PRODUCTS.

**Panel 6:** IS IT A BAD SIGN IF YOU SPEND THE DAY WONDERING WHY THERE ARE NO LAWS AGAINST WHAT YOU DO FOR A LIVING?

**Panel 7:** SALES CONFERENCE. HERE'S THE PRODUCT YOU'LL BE SELLING NEXT QUARTER. IT HAS <u>NO</u> USER INTERFACE!

**Panel 8:** THAT MEANS NO BULKY USER MANUAL. AND NO LOSS OF FUNCTION DURING A POWER OUTAGE!

**Panel 9:** YOU WERE RIGHT. OUR SALES PEOPLE CAN'T DISTINGUISH GOOD FROM EVIL. I STRAINED A SMILE MUSCLE. CLAP CLAP CLAP CLAP

FROM NOW ON, I'LL BE USING THE CHAOS THEORY OF MANAGEMENT.

? ? ?

AND THIS WILL BE DIFFERENT HOW?

NOW THERE'S A NAME FOR IT.

IT TAKES A CERTAIN TYPE OF PERSONALITY TO TELECOMMUTE, DOGBERT.

WHAT?

JUST BECAUSE OTHER PEOPLE HAVE PERSONALITIES DOESN'T MEAN YOU SHOULD TRY TO DEVELOP ONE.

I HAVE A PERSONALITY!

LET'S NOT GET INTO THAT "IS ZERO A NUMBER" DEBATE AGAIN.

I ESTIMATED THE HOURS IT WOULD TAKE TO DO AN EXCELLENT JOB ON ALL THE PROJECTS YOU'VE ASSIGNED.

THAT WOULD BE FIFTY HOURS A DAY. SO I RECALCULATED FOR "ADEQUATE" RESULTS. THAT WOULD BE FORTY HOURS PER DAY.

WELL, TO MAKE A LONG STORY SHORT, LET'S SKIP DOWN TO "COMPLETE FIDUCIARY MISCONDUCT."

BLAH BLAH BLAH BLAH BLAH

34

I JUST READ THAT THE AVERAGE WOMAN IS PAID 75 CENTS FOR EVERY DOLLAR THAT MEN MAKE. IT'S AN OUTRAGE!

I'M THE HIGHEST PAID ENGINEER IN THE COMPANY.

THAT'S IMPOSSIBLE. THE ARTICLE SAYS "AVERAGE WOMEN" EARN LESS.

SUDDENLY, THE PROBLEM COMES INTO FOCUS.

THIS ARTICLE SAYS MEN ARE PAID 25% MORE THAN WOMEN. HOW DO YOU EXPLAIN THAT?

ACTUALLY, IT SAYS WOMEN MAKE 75¢ FOR EVERY DOLLAR THAT MEN MAKE. THAT'S 33% MORE FOR MEN.

I SUPPOSE THERE'S ALMOST NO CHANCE YOU'LL PRAISE ME FOR MY MATH SKILLS RIGHT NOW.

ALICE, ONE DAY I HOPE WE CAN BE JUDGED BY OUR ACCOMPLISHMENTS AND NOT OUR GENDER.

I GOT MY FOURTEENTH PATENT TODAY. I'M ON MY WAY TO A LUNCH BANQUET IN MY HONOR.

AND YOU WORE THAT?

35

OUR USER MANUAL HAS A TYPO. OUR TECHNICAL SUPPORT CALLS ARE GOING TO A PHONE SEX PLACE.

COMPLAINTS ARE WAY DOWN.

CUSTOMER'S HOUSE

WELL, OKAY, BUT... HAS THAT EVER WORKED?

NO COMPLAINTS YET.

I'LL NEED A LETTER OF REFERENCE TO APPLY FOR A JOB IN ANOTHER DIVISION.

NO PROBLEM.

... FOR A MAN OF HIS HYGIENE, HE DOESN'T STEAL AS MUCH AS YOU'D THINK. I SUSPECT HE'S ON DRUGS.

AND THEN HE SAYS YOU'RE PRONE TO ANGER AND DENIAL. IS THAT TRUE?

NO!!

CATBERT: EVIL H.R. DIRECTOR

MY BOSS IS PREVENTING ME FROM TRANSFERING TO A GREAT JOB.

THAT'S OUTRAGEOUS! THERE SHOULDN'T BE ANY GREAT JOBS IN THIS COMPANY.

ONCE AGAIN, YOU'VE MADE A BAD SITUATION WORSE.

THAT'S THE HUMAN RESOURCES PROMISE.

MY NEW PRODUCT IS A DATABASE OF FAMOUS SERIAL KILLERS.

YOU CAN SEARCH THE DATABASE BY NAME, WEAPON OR TATTOO.

LET ME GUESS, WALLY: SIX MONTHS AGO OUR YOUNG INTERN ASKED YOU WHAT THE TERM "KILLER APPLICATION" MEANT.

I CAN REPLACE YOUR CUBICLES WITH "PERSONAL HABITATS."

THEY LOOK EXACTLY LIKE CUBICLES, BUT WE'VE MADE HUGE ADVANCES IN WHAT THEY'RE CALLED.

IS IT EXPENSIVE?

IF MONEY IS AN ISSUE, YOU COULD START WITH THE "HELLHOLE JUNIOR" MODEL AND UPGRADE LATER.

DO YOU HAVE PICTURES?

YOUR CUBICLE HAS BEEN REPLACED BY A "PERSONAL HABITAT."

IT'S EXACTLY LIKE YOUR CUBICLE BUT MUCH LESS CLUTTERED.

HEY, ALL MY STUFF IS IN THE TRASH CAN!

THAT'S A FUNNY THING TO CALL YOUR PERSONAL STORAGE UNIT.

HUMAN RESOURCES IS PRESCRIBING POWERFUL ANTIDEPRESSANTS TO IMPROVE MORALE.

THE LABEL SAYS IT MAY CAUSE "UNWARRANTED OPTIMISM ABOUT YOUR DEAD-END JOB."

I GOTTA GET ME SOME OF THAT.

LOOK AT THE WARNING LABEL ON ALICE'S ANTIDEPRESSANTS.

IT CAN CAUSE FATIGUE, DISORIENTATION, MEMORY LOSS, AND LACK OF SEX.

I WONDER HOW LONG WE'VE BEEN TAKING THEM.

THERE'S NO WAY TO KNOW.

ALICE IS OVERDOSING ON ANTIDEPRESSANTS.

WE MUST INDUCE VOMITING.

LOOK AT OUR MISSION STATEMENT, ALICE. THE PEOPLE WHO WROTE IT EARN TEN TIMES YOUR SALARY.

THE PLAN WORKED PERFECTLY, UP TO THE POINT WHERE ALL THREE OF US WERE HEAVING AND ALICE WAS PUNCHING US.

Panel 1: I AM MORDAC, THE PREVENTER OF INFORMATION SERVICES. I BRING NEW GUIDELINES FOR PASSWORDS.

Panel 2: "ALL PASSWORDS MUST BE AT LEAST SIX CHARACTERS LONG... INCLUDE NUMBERS AND LETTERS... INCLUDE A MIX OF UPPER AND LOWER CASE..."

Panel 3: SQUEAL LIKE A PIG!!! "USE DIFFERENT PASSWORDS FOR EACH SYSTEM. CHANGE ONCE A MONTH. DO NOT WRITE ANYTHING DOWN."

Panel 4: I AM MORDAC, THE PREVENTER OF INFORMATION SERVICES. I COME TO CONFISCATE YOUR NON-STANDARD COMPUTER.

Panel 5: YOU'LL GIVE ME A NEW ONE, RIGHT? THIS IS HEAVIER THAN IT LOOKS.

Panel 6: I'LL HAVE TO DISABLE IT AND LEAVE IT HERE. THE NEW ONE IS ALREADY ON ITS WAY, RIGHT?

Panel 7: REQUEST DENIED. THE INFORMATION SERVICES DEPARTMENT DOES NOT UPGRADE NON-STANDARD COMPUTERS.

Panel 8: IT'S NOT AN UPGRADE. IT'S A REPLACEMENT. OUR POLICY IS THAT IT'S AN UPGRADE UNLESS YOU DISCARD THE OLD ONE.

Panel 9: YOUR TRASH IS DECLINED. OUR POLICY IS "NO COMPUTERS."

S.Adams

4/6/98 4/7/98 4/8/98

49

**DOGBERT THE CONSULTANT**

I CAN GIVE YOU EXCELLENT ADVICE FOR $50,000 PER MONTH...

IF BUDGET IS A PROBLEM, I ALSO OFFER <u>BAD</u> ADVICE FOR THE LOW PRICE OF $45,000 PER MONTH.

THAT'S NOT A GOOD SIGN.

I SAVED A LOT OF MONEY BY HIRING A LOW-PRICED CONSULTANT.

THESE AREN'T THE BEST RECOMMENDATIONS IN THE WORLD, BUT THE PRICE WAS VERY REASONABLE.

I DON'T LIKE THIS ONE ABOUT ROLLING AROUND ON UNWASHED HAMBURGER PATTIES.

KEEP AN OPEN MIND.

ALTHOUGH YOUR COMPANY IS VERY PROFITABLE, I WOULDN'T BE MUCH OF A CONSULTANT IF I DIDN'T RECOMMEND CHANGES.

YOU RECOMMEND JAILING OUR OMBUDSMAN AND DECLARING MARTIAL LAW... MAKES SENSE.

THEN COULD I SHOOT EMPLOYEES WHO MAKE PERSONAL PHONE CALLS?

IT'S OKAY WITH ME.

AS A CONSULTANT, I'M OVERPAID EVEN IF I DO BAD WORK.

WHEREAS YOU'RE UNDERPAID EVEN IF YOU DO GOOD WORK.

IT'S FUNNY IF YOU THINK ABOUT IT.

I MIGHT HAVE A TERRIBLE JOB, BUT AT LEAST I DON'T HAVE ANY JOB SECURITY.

ALICE, I CHECKED WITH THE OTHER MANAGERS; THEY DON'T KNOW YOU WELL ENOUGH TO PROMOTE YOU.

SO WE'VE DECIDED TO HIRE SOMEONE FROM OUTSIDE THE COMPANY.

AT LEAST THE OTHER MANAGERS HAVE HEARD MY NAME NOW.

I DIDN'T USE YOUR REAL NAME.

CATBERT: EVIL H.R. DIRECTOR

I'M HAVING TROUBLE FINDING QUALIFIED EXTERNAL APPLICANTS.

ALL I HAVE ARE A HEADLESS MAN, A MIME, AND A FROZEN CRO-MAGNON GUY WE FOUND IN A GLACIER.

DOES THE MIME BRING HIS OWN INVISIBLE CUBICLE? I LOVE THOSE!

ONLY IF WE PAY HIS RELOCATION COSTS.

MAYBE IT WAS WRONG TO PROMISE OUR CUSTOMERS A PRODUCT THAT HASN'T BEEN DESIGNED YET.

BUT OUR MOTTO IN MARKETING IS, "IT'S BETTER TO ASK FOR FORGIVENESS THAN TO SEEK PERMISSION."

YOUR MOTTO NEEDS SOME DESIGN WORK TOO.

I DONATED A BILLION DOLLARS TO THE UNITED NATIONS TODAY.

THAT'S NICE OF YOU.

MY ONLY CONDITION IS THAT THEY NAME SOMETHING AFTER ME.

UNITED NATIONS

FOR THE MILLIONTH TIME: YES, I'M SURE WE WANT TO KEEP CALLING IT FRANCE!

FRANCE

ALICE, YOU'D GET MORE ACCOMPLISHED IF YOU WERE LESS OF A PERFECTIONIST.

I'VE ASKED WALLY TO WORK WITH YOU — TO TEACH YOU HOW TO BE LESS PERFECT.

WHEN DID APATHY AND LOW STANDARDS BECOME POSITIVE TRAITS?

I CALL IT THE INTRAPRENEUR-IAL SPIRIT.

57

THE COMPANY IS GIVING FREE FLU SHOTS, WALLY.

THE SHOTS WILL BE DELIVERED BY WEALTHY STOCKHOLDERS WHO WILL HUNT YOU DOWN AND SHOOT YOU WITH FLU DARTS.

AT LEAST I WON'T GET THE FLU, RIGHT?

YOU'RE PROBABLY THINKING OF THE FLU PREVENTION SHOTS.

NO ONE LIKES BEING HUNTED DOWN AND SHOT WITH FLU DARTS, WALLY.

BUT REMEMBER: COMPANIES ARE MANAGED FOR THE BENEFIT OF STOCKHOLDERS, NOT EMPLOYEES.

I OWN STOCK. IT'S IN MY 401(K) ACCOUNT.

I'M NOT SUPPOSED TO TELL YOU, BUT NONE OF THAT IS REAL.

I HAD TO MAKE SOME OPTIMISTIC ASSUMPTIONS TO MEET THE REVENUE TARGET.

IN WEEK THREE, WE'RE VISITED BY AN ALIEN NAMED D'UTOX INAG WHO OFFERS TO SHARE HIS ADVANCED TECHNOLOGY.

THEN DO WE USE HIS TECHNOLOGY TO DESIGN OUR NEW PRODUCT?

NO, WE KILL HIM AND SELL THE AUTOPSY VIDEO.

I'M CREATING A COMIC STRIP CALLED "PIPPY THE ZIPHEAD."

I'M CRAMMING AS MUCH ARTWORK IN THERE AS POSSIBLE, SO NO ONE WILL NOTICE THERE'S ONLY ONE JOKE.

THE JOKE IS ON THE READER, ISN'T IT?

I'D BETTER CRAM SOME MORE ART IN THERE.

YOUR COMIC STRIP SEEMS TO BE NOTHING BUT A CLOWN WITH A SMALL HEAD WHO SAYS RANDOM THINGS.

THAT'S PIPPY.

I'M MAINTAINING MY ARTISTIC INTEGRITY BY CREATING A COMIC THAT NO ONE WILL ENJOY.

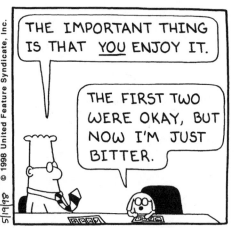

THE IMPORTANT THING IS THAT YOU ENJOY IT.

THE FIRST TWO WERE OKAY, BUT NOW I'M JUST BITTER.

DILBERT, THIS IS ALLEN, MY NEW SYCOPHANT.

HIS HEAD NODS WHENEVER I TALK. BUT THAT'S NOT THE BEST PART...

VERY IMPRESSIVE.

IS THAT GREAT OR WHAT?

I WILL NOW TEST MY THEORY THAT PEOPLE LIKE TO BE TOLD WHAT TO DO.

QUIT YOUR JOB AND BUILD ME A PYRAMID, YOU HOMELY DOLT!!!

TECH

I LIKED IT UNTIL THE DOLT PART.

I'VE NOTICED THAT HONESTY DOESN'T MIX WELL WITH ANYTHING.

WHAT'S THE CROWN FOR?

THERE AREN'T ANY CHARISMATIC LEADERS IN THE WORLD LATELY. I'M GOING TO FILL THE VOID.

DON'T CHARISMATIC LEADERS USUALLY TURN OUT TO BE EGOMANIACAL, PHILANDERING SOCIOPATHS?

AND THEY LOOK GOOD IN HATS!

WHY ARE THERE NO CHARISMATIC LEADERS ANYMORE?

CABLE TV.

SCANDAL IS THE MOST ECONOMICAL WAY TO FILL NEWS PROGRAMS. THEY'LL GO AFTER YOU, TOO.

I'LL NEED A DIVERSION.

I DON'T CARE IF IT'S A GREAT NEWS STORY; I WILL NOT TAKE FERTILITY DRUGS!

THEY'RE IN YOUR COFFEE.

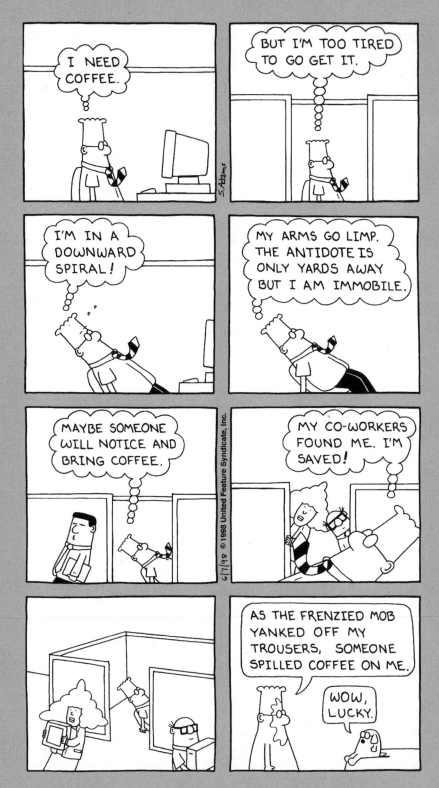

70

CATBERT: EVIL H.R. DIRECTOR

BAD NEWS: THE EMPLOYEES ARE READING A NEWSPAPER.

IF THEY SEE THE LOW UNEMPLOYMENT RATE, THEY'LL KNOW THE BALANCE OF POWER HAS SWUNG THEIR WAY.

I PLAN TO USE THE CAT AS A GARGOYLE ON MY CUBICLE ROOF.

IF YOU RUN A CURRENT THROUGH HIM YOU CAN ZAP BUGS.

THIS WEEK I DISCOVERED THAT THE DEMAND FOR ENGINEERS EXCEEDS THE SUPPLY.

I RESPONDED BY INCREASING MY INSOLENCE AND DECREASING MY PRODUCTIVITY.

I WILL NEVER HIRE ANOTHER ENGINEER AS LONG AS I'M ALIVE.

EQUILIBRIUM HAS BEEN RESTORED.

YOUR CUBICLE ROOF IS LOOKING GOOD.

YEP.

I LOVE BEING A SKILLED WORKER IN A PERIOD OF LOW UNEMPLOYMENT. I CAN GET ANYTHING I DEMAND.

HEY, POINDEXTER, FETCH ME A LEMONADE.

POINK

OUCH

UNLIKE YOU PEOPLE IN MARKETING, I HAVE HIGHLY SOUGHT TECHNICAL SKILLS.

I'M TOO VALUABLE TO FIRE. SO FROM NOW ON, I'LL DELIVER MY PROJECT STATUS ON A BALLED-UP PIECE OF PAPER.

IS THE CHEERLEADER SQUAD READY?

GRRR.

I'D LIKE TO REOPEN THE QUESTION OF WHAT VENDOR WE'LL USE, EVEN THOUGH IT'S TOO LATE TO CHANGE ANYTHING.

I DARN YOU TO HECK! YOU WILL SPEND AN ETERNITY WITH OTHER INDECISIVE DULLARDS!

WHERE ARE YOU TAKING ME??!

HERE IS FINE.

DANGEROUS ASBESTOS HAS BEEN FOUND IN EVERY ROOM IN OUR BUILDING.

THE PROBLEM WILL BE ADDRESSED USING A ... SCIENTIFIC PROCESS.

SOMETHING CALLED ATTRITION.

NO ONE IN MY DIVISION IS USING THE COMPANY DRUG TREATMENT PROGRAM. THIS IS VERY EMBARRASSING.

MY BOSS WILL THINK I'M NOT MANAGING THE DRUG PROBLEM. DON'T <u>ANY</u> OF YOU HAVE A DRUG PROBLEM?

#!*%☁ CHILDPROOF "MIDOL" CONTAINER!!

HMM...

DRUG TREATMENT PROGRAM

THE FIRST STEP IS TO ADMIT YOU HAVE A DRUG PROBLEM.

I DON'T

MY POINTY-HAIRED BOSS FORCED ME TO BE HERE BECAUSE HE THINKS IT MAKES HIM LOOK PROACTIVE.

HALLUCINATIONS ARE COMMON DURING WITHDRAWAL. LET'S DO AN INKBLOTCH TEST.

AAAGH!!

DRUG TREATMENT PROGRAM

ALICE, I'D LIKE TO TALK TO YOU ABOUT YOUR REGISTRATION FORM.

UNDER "OBJECTIVE," YOU SAID YOU WANT TO USE MY "TURNIP-SHAPED HEAD AS A BATTERING RAM TO BREAK OUT OF HERE."

ALICE, DROP THE DUCT TAPE.

STAY TENSE; THAT WILL HELP.

74

76

MISTER DOGBERT HAS RETURNED AS OUR C.E.O. BECAUSE NO ONE ELSE WANTS THE JOB.

I CAN'T TELL YOU MY PLAN FOR THE ASSETS OF THIS COMPANY ... BUT IT RHYMES WITH "VILLAGE."

I HOPE IT'S "FILLAGE."

DOGBERT THE C.E.O.

I NEED A PERSONAL "GOPHER." ARE YOU INTERESTED?

SURE!

GOOD. YOU'LL WEAR A SPECIAL UNIFORM AND HAVE A SPECIAL OFFICE TO SHOW YOUR STATUS.

SHEESH. I HAVEN'T MADE A BANK SHOT YET.

DOGBERT THE C.E.O.

I'VE DECIDED TO MANIPULATE OUR STOCK PRICE FOR PERSONAL GAIN.

I'LL SPIN OFF A FEW DIVISIONS, BUY BACK SOME OF OUR STOCK AND ANNOUNCE MASSIVE BUDGET CUTS.

UM... DO YOU EVEN KNOW WHAT PRODUCTS WE MAKE?

HOW WOULD THAT BE RELEVANT?

DOGBERT'S TECH SUPPORT

HOW MAY I ABUSE YOU?

THE INTERNET IS SLOW. WHAT CAUSES THAT?

THAT CAN ONLY BE CAUSED BY YOU LOOKING AT PORN.

I'LL NEED YOUR NAME FOR OUR RECORDS.

CLICK

7/2/98

I LIKE MEN WHO HAVE A SENSE OF HUMOR.

...BUT NOT THE JOKE-TELLING KIND — THE SPONTANEOUS KIND — LIKE WHEN YOU SPILL SOMETHING AND WE BOTH LAUGH.

7/3/98

MAYBE I'M TRYING TOO HARD.

I DON'T UNDERSTAND WHY YOU LIKE THE THINGS YOU LIKE.

I'M FORCED TO CONCLUDE THAT YOU'RE SOCIALLY DEFECTIVE.

7/4/98

ISN'T IT NORMAL FOR PEOPLE TO HAVE UNIQUE PREFERENCES?

DO YOU HAVE TO ARGUE WITH EVERYTHING I SAY?!

CATBERT: H.R. DIRECTOR

"CONSISTENT WITH OUR EFFORT TO ELIMINATE PRIVACY AND DIGNITY..."

"...EMPLOYEES MUST SHARE HOTEL ROOMS ON ALL BUSINESS TRIPS."

AFTER THEY GET USED TO THIS, I'LL INTRODUCE THE TANDEM SHOWERING POLICY.

WALLY, AS YOU KNOW, EMPLOYEES MUST SHARE HOTEL ROOMS AT THE CONFERENCE...

SO I WAS WONDERING IF YOU'D LIKE TO... YOU KNOW... BE MY ROOMIE.

SURE.

WE'LL HAVE TO AGREE ON SOME RULES.

I CAN ONLY SPOON ON MY RIGHT.

I HATE SHARING A HOTEL ROOM ON BUSINESS TRIPS.

I NEED TO DO MY EXERCISES BEFORE I GO TO SLEEP. DO YOU MIND?

THERE ARE SO MANY WAYS THAT THIS COULD BE BAD.

I'M STILL A BIT WINDED FROM YESTERDAY.

SHARING A HOTEL ROOM

I FORGOT TO PACK MY EXERCISE SHORTS.

I GUESS I CAN DO MY JUMPING JACKS WITHOUT CLOTHES. IT'S JUST US GUYS.

SINGLE OCCUPANCY ISN'T SO HARD TO GET.

I DON'T SEE WHY OUR WEB PAGES NEED URLS. GET RID OF THEM.

DID THAT MAKE ANY SENSE AT ALL?

YES, IT'S BRILLIANT.

GIVE ME A MONTH AND I'LL REPLACE OUR URLS WITH UNIFORM RESOURCE LOCATORS.

PERFECT.

I'M PLEASED TO REPORT ANOTHER STELLAR WEEK OF ACCOMPLISHMENTS!

I MOVED MORE THAN 800,000 BITS OF DATA TO A DISASTER RECOVERY BACK-UP FACILITY!

DID YOU JUST TAKE CREDIT FOR COPYING A FILE TO A DISKETTE?

IT WAS MY RÉSUMÉ.

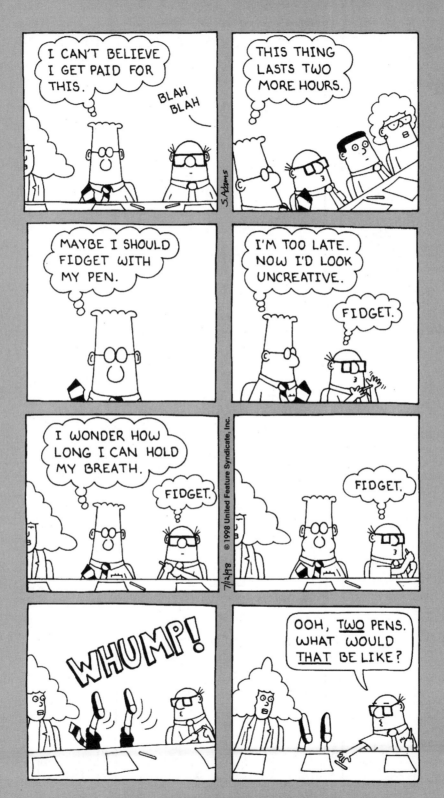

I HIRED MY SON TO MANAGE OUR TECHNOLOGY DEVELOPMENT GROUP.

HE'S YOUNG, BUT I'M ALMOST POSITIVE HE WENT TO COLLEGE.

WHERE DID YOU GO TO COLLEGE?

ACTUALLY, I HID IN OUR ATTIC FOR FOUR YEARS.

MY DAD TAUGHT ME EVERYTHING I KNOW.

HE USED TO SAY "DON'T DRINK THE PICKLE JUICE UNTIL THE PICKLES ARE GONE."

WAS THAT A BIG PROBLEM AT YOUR HOUSE?

HAVE YOU EVER BEEN HIT IN THE EYE WITH A PICKLE?

SON-OF-A-BOSS

YOU HAVE TO MAKE OUR PRODUCT SO SIMPLE THAT MY MOM COULD USE IT.

IT'S ALREADY SO SIMPLE A HAMSTER COULD USE IT. HOW MUCH DUMBER IS YOUR MOM?

MAYBE WE SHOULD LEAVE MY MOM OUT OF THIS.

MY MOM IS A PHYSICIST.

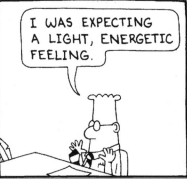

90

MY BOSS TOLD ME TO BUY A BUNCH OF EQUIPMENT WE DON'T NEED.

THAT WAY OUR BUDGET WON'T GET CUT NEXT YEAR.

I'M SO PROUD OF YOU, SON.

HOW DO YOU SAY THAT WITH A STRAIGHT FACE?

I TRY TO IMAGINE YOU AS A NAVY SEAL.

...AND WE'LL BUY A DOZEN OF THESE. WE'RE TRYING TO SPEND OUR BUDGET SO IT DOESN'T GET CUT NEXT YEAR.

THIS IS GREAT! YOU GUYS ARE SO DUMB THAT I DON'T EVEN HAVE TO USE MY FAKE PERSONALITY TO MAKE THE SALE!

...AND NINE OF THESE BLUE THINGS.

THERE'S A FULL MOON ON THE HORIZON!

I HAVEN'T TALKED YET, BUT ALL THE GOOD POINTS HAVE BEEN TAKEN.

BLAH BLAH

BLAH BLAH

WE MUST MAKE SURE OUR MOMENTUM ALIGNS WITH OUR VALUE-ADDED DISTRIBUTION!

THAT WAS JUST BABBLE, RIGHT?

ALL THE GOOD ONES WERE TAKEN.

94

WE WON THE BID TO CREATE A DIGITAL ARCHIVE OF THE WORLD'S GREATEST ART.

THIS WILL GIVE US A CHANCE TO FIX ANY ERRORS MADE BY THE ARTISTS.

ERRORS?

FOR EXAMPLE, THERE WAS A GUY WHO USED TOO MUCH BLUE FOR A WHOLE PERIOD.

WE'VE DIGITIZED AND INDEXED THE WORLD'S GREATEST ART. THIS IS "THE LAST SUPPER."

NICE, BUT...

THE COMPOSITION IS CLUTTERED. DELETE A FEW OF THOSE GUYS. DO YOU HAVE ANY CLIP ART OF BAGELS?

DO THEY LOOK HAPPY?

COMPARED TO ME, YES.

I'M CREATING A DIGITAL ARCHIVE OF THE WORLD'S GREATEST ART. BUT MY BOSS INSISTS ON "FIXING" THE ARTISTS' MISTAKES.

HEE HEE

THIS IS SUCH A FUNNY STORY FOR THE NEWSLETTER!

IT'S A FUNNY STORY, BUT CHANGE "FIXING" TO "DRAMATICALLY IMPROVING."

97

NASA PUT ALL THE WOMEN WHO LOVE ENGINEERS ON THE MOON. THEY SAY IT'S AN IMPORTANT EXPERIMENT.

EVERY WEEKEND THEY SEND A SHUTTLE FULL OF MALE NASA ENGINEERS TO CHECK ON OUR STATUS.

UH-OH. WE HAVE COMPANY.

SOMEWHERE ON THE MOON

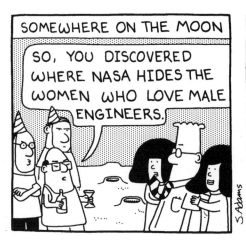

SO, YOU DISCOVERED WHERE NASA HIDES THE WOMEN WHO LOVE MALE ENGINEERS.

HOW ABOUT A LITTLE DRINKING CONTEST, TOUGH GUY? THE LOSER CAN NEVER RETURN.

WE PROBABLY SHOULDN'T HAVE INSISTED ON ENTERING THE CONTEST.

I'LL MISS THEM.

I NEED THIS VITAL INFORMATION BY ONE O'CLOCK.

IF I DO A SHODDY JOB, I CAN FINISH THIS AND STILL MAKE IT TO LUNCH!

TODAY I TRADED MY WORK ETHIC FOR A BANANA.

I ATE THAT BANANA YEARS AGO.

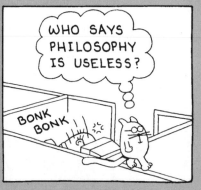

THIS IS TODAY'S MOTIVATIONAL MESSAGE FOR ALL EMPLOYEES.

TODAY IS THE FIRST DAY OF THE REST OF THE WEEK.

OR IS IT?

WALLY, DID YOU REVIEW MY DRAFT OF THE USER MANUAL YET?

THE CHARACTERS IN THE EXAMPLES GAVE ME NO REASON TO CARE ABOUT THEM. IT LEFT ME EMPTY.

SADLY, USER "B" COULD NEVER LOVE USER "A" BECAUSE HE WAS A BALD ENGINEER.

CATBERT: EVIL H.R. DIRECTOR

YOU'VE BEEN A GOOD CONTRACT EMPLOYEE. WE'D LIKE TO MAKE YOU A REGULAR EMPLOYEE.

YOU MEAN YOU WANT TO PAY ME LESS?

WE WANT YOU TO BE MOTIVATED BY SOMETHING OTHER THAN MONEY.

LIKE... STUPIDITY?

CATBERT: EVIL H.R. DIRECTOR

YES, REGULAR EMPLOYEES ARE PAID LESS THAN CONTRACT EMPLOYEES SUCH AS YOURSELF.

BUT IF YOU JOIN THE COMPANY, YOU'LL GET MANY INTANGIBLE BENEFITS.

MAYBE YOUR STOCK-HOLDERS WOULD LIKE SOME INTANGIBLE BENEFITS. THEY CAN HAVE MINE.

THE EMPLOYEES AREN'T FALLING FOR THE OLD "INTANGIBLE BENEFITS" STORY ANYMORE.

UH-OH. WE DON'T EARN ENOUGH MONEY TO GIVE TANGIBLE BENEFITS TO EMPLOYEES AND STOCKHOLDERS.

STOCKHOLDER MEETING

STOCK

... NOW LET'S DISCUSS YOUR INTANGIBLE BENEFITS...

%#!

HERE'S MY TIME SHEET, IN EXQUISITE DETAIL.

CRINKLE CRINKLE WAD

IT'S EASIER TO INPUT THE NUMBERS IF I MAKE THEM UP AS I GO.

I LIKE TO CON PEOPLE. AND I LIKE TO INSULT PEOPLE.

IF YOU COMBINE CON AND INSULT, YOU GET "CONSULT."

I'M HERE TO CONSULT YOU.

IT SOUNDS EXPENSIVE AND DEMEANING. ... OKAY.

DOGBERT CONSULTS

MY RECOMMENDATIONS ARE BASED ON AN ANALYSIS OF ACCOUNTABILITY.

OOH.

AS A CONSULTANT, I'M NOT ACCOUNTABLE TO YOUR STOCKHOLDERS. SO I CAN RECOMMEND ANYTHING THAT AMUSES ME.

I RECOMMEND THAT YOU CONVERT ALL OF YOUR U.S. DOLLARS TO ELBONIAN CURRENCY... WHATEVER THAT IS.

THE EYE-CRUD.

YOUR PERFORMANCE WAS EXCELLENT, BUT THERE'S NO BONUS THIS YEAR.

WHY NOT?

THE COMPANY LOST A FORTUNE IN THE ELBONIAN CURRENCY COLLAPSE.

BUT IN A WAY, IT'S YOUR OWN FAULT FOR WORKING HERE.

THANKS. THAT TAKES THE STING OUT.

RATBERT THE CONSULTANT

I'M MAKING $200,000 PER YEAR!

APPARENTLY THAT'S ALL I KNOW.

THANKS TO MY CONSULTING JOB, I'M WEALTHIER THAN YOU.

AND I'M CUTER, OBVIOUSLY. THE ONLY THING LEFT IS PERSONALITY.

SHOULDN'T YOU BE SPREADING DISEASE SOMEWHERE?

THREE FOR THREE! YES!!

I BUILT A RING WITH A TINY COMPUTER IN IT.

IT ONLY DISPLAYS ONE CHARACTER AT A TIME.

THEN WHAT GOOD IS IT?

NO TIME FOR CHIT-CHAT. I'M SURFIN' THE NET!

DON'T MAKE ME COME OVER THERE.

I GOT CAUGHT IN TRAFFIC.

LET ME RECAP WHAT YOU MISSED. WE SPENT THE PAST HOUR DECIDING NOT TO CHANGE THE NAME OF OUR DEPARTMENT.

YOU JUST INADVERTENTLY TRAINED ME TO BE LATE TO ALL MEETINGS.

OOPS.

I'VE BEEN BUILDING UP MY FOREARM SO I'LL HAVE A BONE-CRUSHING HANDSHAKE.

WHY?

HEY, WHAT'S THIS — SOME SORT OF HEN PARTY?

THAT WAS VERY WITTY, WALLY. CONGRATULATIONS!

OH.

THE SAFETY AWARD GOES TO TED FOR HIS FIVE YEARS OF INJURY-FREE WORK.

THANK YOU FOR THIS AWARD. WITHOUT AWARDS, THERE WOULD BE NO INCENTIVE TO AVOID INJURIES.

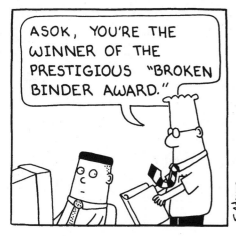

FROM NOW ON, ANYONE WHO MISSES A STAFF MEETING MUST BUY DONUTS FOR THE NEXT MEETING.

DID I JUST SELL THEM THEIR FREEDOM FOR DONUTS?

HERE'S ANOTHER SHOVEL FULL OF ASSIGNMENTS.

HOW AM I SUPPOSED TO GET ALL OF THAT DONE?

ONLY DO THE MOST IMPORTANT ONES.

"IDENTIFY ALL THE ACRONYMS THAT HAVE NEVER BEEN USED."

THAT'S AN IMPORTANT ONE.

I HAVE TIME TO DO ONE OF THESE TWO ASSIGNMENTS.

ONE IS ESSENTIAL TO THE BUSINESS. THE OTHER IS NOT. WHICH ONE DO YOU WANT ME TO DO?

BOTH!

I KNOW YOU WANT BOTH. BUT IF YOU CAN ONLY GET ONE...

COMBINE THEM AND JUST DO THE ONE.

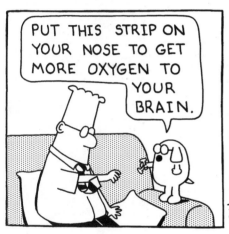

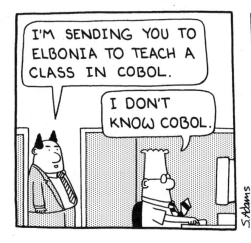

DILBERT TEACHES COBOL IN ELBONIA

...AND THAT'S HOW YOU FIX YOUR "YEAR 2000" PROBLEM.

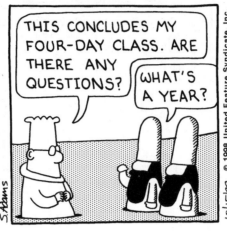

THIS CONCLUDES MY FOUR-DAY CLASS. ARE THERE ANY QUESTIONS?

WHAT'S A YEAR?

AND IS COBOL A KIND OF CABBAGE OR WHAT?

CLASS DISMISSED.

CATBERT THE H.R. DIRECTOR

ASOK, IT'S TIME TO GROOM YOU FOR MANAGEMENT.

I DON'T SEE TOO MANY BUGS IN YOUR FUR.

CAN YOU LICK THE TOP OF YOUR OWN HEAD?

NO, I CAN'T.

THEN YOU CAN'T BE A MANAGER.

WE'LL TAKE AWAY THE CUBICLE WALLS AND FORCE EMPLOYEES TO WORK IN AN "OPEN PLAN" OFFICE.

SURVEILLANCE CAMERAS WILL RECORD THEIR EVERY MOVE. WE'LL MONITOR PHONE CALLS AND WEB USE. WE'LL EVEN TEST THEIR BLOOD!

CAN WE FLOG THEM?

WHOA, COWBOY! WAIT FOR PHASE TWO.